This Travel Journal Belongs To:

AREA *Suggestions*

LOCAL TOWNS:

Mendoza City

Luján de Cuyo

San Carlos

Chacras de Coria

Maipú

Tunuyán

Las Heras

San José

Godoy Cruz

Wineries Often Require Reservations & Many Only Take Cash

MAJOR WINE REGIONS:

Uco Valley

Luján de Cuyo

Maipú

THINGS TO DO & SEE:

Mendoza Wine Tours

Reserva Natural Villavicencio

Horseback Ride Through the Valley

Hike Cerra Aconcagua

Plaza Independencia

Aconcagua Provincial Park

Museo Nacional Del Vino y la Vendimia

Parque San Martin

Baccus Biking – Wine Tours

Go White-Water Rafting

Puente del Inca

Cacheuta Thermal Baths

Cerro de la Gloria

Nightlife on Calle Arístides

Tupungato

MENDOZA *Bucket List*

PLACES I WANT TO VISIT:

THINGS I WANT TO DO:

TOP 3 DESTINATIONS:

TRAVEL *Planner*

DESTINATION:	DATES:

BUDGET:	WEATHER:	CURRENCY EXCHANGE:

ACCOMODATION OVERVIEW

NAME:	LOCATION:	DATE:	ADDRESS:

NOTES & TRAVEL DETAILS

TRIP BUDGET *Planner*

TRIP DETAILS:

AMOUNT NEEDED:

OUR GOAL DATE:

DEPOSIT TRACKER

AMOUNT DEPOSITED: **DATE DEPOSITED:**

TRAVEL EXPENSE *Tracker*

DESTINATION: _____   BUDGET GOAL: _____

DATE:	DESCRIPTION:	CURRENCY:	AMOUNT:

TOTAL EXPENSES:

TRAVEL EXPENSE *Tracker*

DESTINATION: _____   BUDGET GOAL: _____

DATE:	DESCRIPTION:	CURRENCY:	AMOUNT:

TOTAL EXPENSES:

FLIGHT *Information*

DATE: DESTINATION:

AIRLINE:	
BOOKING NUMBER:	
DEPARTURE DATE:	
BOARDING TIME:	
GATE NUMBER:	
SEAT NUMBER:	
FLIGHT DURATION:	
ARRIVAL / LANDING TIME:	

DATE: DESTINATION:

AIRLINE:	
BOOKING NUMBER:	
DEPARTURE DATE:	
BOARDING TIME:	
GATE NUMBER:	
SEAT NUMBER:	
FLIGHT DURATION:	
ARRIVAL / LANDING TIME:	

TRAIN *Information*

DATE: _____   DESTINATION: _____

TRAIN PASS (EURAIL, ETC.):	
DEPARTING STATION:	
DEPARTURE DATE:	
BOARDING TIME:	
GATE NUMBER:	
SEAT NUMBER:	
ARRIVAL STATION:	
ARRIVAL / LANDING TIME:	

DATE: _____   DESTINATION: _____

TRAIN PASS (EURAIL, ETC.):	
DEPARTING STATION:	
DEPARTURE DATE:	
BOARDING TIME:	
GATE NUMBER:	
SEAT NUMBER:	
ARRIVAL STATION:	
ARRIVAL / LANDING TIME:	

TRAIN *Information*

DATE: DESTINATION:

TRAIN PASS (EURAIL, ETC.):	
DEPARTING STATION:	
DEPARTURE DATE:	
BOARDING TIME:	
GATE NUMBER:	
SEAT NUMBER:	
ARRIVAL STATION:	
ARRIVAL / LANDING TIME:	

DATE: DESTINATION:

TRAIN PASS (EURAIL, ETC.):	
DEPARTING STATION:	
DEPARTURE DATE:	
BOARDING TIME:	
GATE NUMBER:	
SEAT NUMBER:	
ARRIVAL STATION:	
ARRIVAL / LANDING TIME:	

VEHICLE *Information*

TYPE: PERSONAL RENTAL

CAR RENTAL AGENCY:	
CONTACT INFORMATION:	
PICK UP DATE AND TIME:	
RETURN DATE AND TIME:	
MAKE & MODEL:	
INSPECTION NOTES:	
COST PER DAY:	
TOTAL COST:	

TYPE: GUIDED TOUR RENTAL

TOUR BUS RENTAL:	
TOUR COMPANY CONTACT:	
TOUR GUIDE NAME:	
DEPARTURE DATE AND TIME:	
LOCATIONS TO BE VISITED:	
COST PER TICKET:	
TOTAL COST FOR GROUP:	

TRAVEL *Planner*

PRE-TRAVEL CHECKLIST

1 MONTH BEFORE

- [ ]
- [ ]
- [ ]
- [ ]
- [ ]

2 WEEKS BEFORE

- [ ]
- [ ]
- [ ]
- [ ]
- [ ]

1 WEEK BEFORE

- [ ]
- [ ]
- [ ]
- [ ]
- [ ]

2 DAYS BEFORE

- [ ]
- [ ]
- [ ]
- [ ]
- [ ]

24 HOURS BEFORE

- [ ]
- [ ]
- [ ]
- [ ]
- [ ]

DAY OF TRAVEL

- [ ]
- [ ]
- [ ]
- [ ]
- [ ]

TRIP TO DO *List*

PACKING *Check List*

DOCUMENTS

- ☐ PASSPORT
- ☐ DRIVER'S LICENSE
- ☐ VISA
- ☐ PLANE TICKETS
- ☐ LOCAL CURRENCY
- ☐ INSURANCE CARD
- ☐ HEALTH CARD
- ☐ OTHER ID
- ☐ HOTEL INFO
- ☐ _____

CLOTHING

- ☐ SOCKS
- ☐ SWIM WEAR
- ☐ T-SHIRTS
- ☐ JEANS/PANTS
- ☐ SHORTS
- ☐ SKIRTS / DRESSES
- ☐ JACKET / COAT
- ☐ SLEEPWEAR
- ☐ SHOES
- ☐ _____

PERSONAL ITEMS

- ☐ SHAMPOO
- ☐ RAZORS
- ☐ COSMETICS
- ☐ HAIR BRUSH
- ☐ LIP BALM
- ☐ WATER BOTTLE
- ☐ SOAP
- ☐ TOOTHBRUSH
- ☐ JEWELRY
- ☐ _____

ELECTRONICS

- ☐ CELL PHONE
- ☐ CHARGER
- ☐ LAPTOP
- ☐ BATTERIES
- ☐ EARPHONES
- ☐ CAMERA
- ☐ MEMORY CARD
- ☐ _____
- ☐ _____
- ☐ _____

HEALTH & SAFETY

- ☐ HAND SANITIZER
- ☐ SUNSCREEN
- ☐ VITAMIN
- ☐ BANDAIDS
- ☐ ADVIL/TYLENOL
- ☐ GLASSES
- ☐ COLD/FLU MEDS
- ☐ _____
- ☐ _____
- ☐ _____

ESSENTIALS

- ☐ _____
- ☐ _____
- ☐ _____
- ☐ _____
- ☐ _____
- ☐ _____
- ☐ _____
- ☐ _____
- ☐ _____
- ☐ _____

PACKING *Check List*

DATE OF TRIP: **DURATION:**

OUTFIT *Planner*

DAY: _____ DESTINATION: _____ PACKED: ☐

DAY: _____

ACTIVITY: _____

OUTFIT: _____

SHOES: _____

ACC: _____

EVENING: _____

DAY: _____ DESTINATION: _____ PACKED: ☐

DAY: _____

ACTIVITY: _____

OUTFIT: _____

SHOES: _____

ACC: _____

EVENING: _____

DAY: _____ DESTINATION: _____ PACKED: ☐

DAY: _____

ACTIVITY: _____

OUTFIT: _____

SHOES: _____

ACC: _____

EVENING: _____

OUTFIT *Planner*

DAY: DESTINATION: PACKED:

      DAY: EVENING:

ACTIVITY:

OUTFIT:

SHOES:

ACC:

DAY: DESTINATION: PACKED:

      DAY: EVENING:

ACTIVITY:

OUTFIT:

SHOES:

ACC:

DAY: DESTINATION: PACKED:

      DAY: EVENING:

ACTIVITY:

OUTFIT:

SHOES:

ACC:

OUTFIT *Planner*

DAY: DESTINATION: PACKED: ☐

DAY: EVENING:

ACTIVITY:

OUTFIT:

SHOES:

ACC:

DAY: DESTINATION: PACKED: ☐

DAY: EVENING:

ACTIVITY:

OUTFIT:

SHOES:

ACC:

DAY: DESTINATION: PACKED: ☐

DAY: EVENING:

ACTIVITY:

OUTFIT:

SHOES:

ACC:

OUTFIT *Planner*

DAY: DESTINATION: PACKED: ☐

                DAY: EVENING:

ACTIVITY:

OUTFIT:

SHOES:

ACC:

DAY: DESTINATION: PACKED: ☐

                DAY: EVENING:

ACTIVITY:

OUTFIT:

SHOES:

ACC:

DAY: DESTINATION: PACKED: ☐

                DAY: EVENING:

ACTIVITY:

OUTFIT:

SHOES:

ACC:

OUTFIT *Planner*

DAY: DESTINATION: PACKED: ☐

DAY: EVENING:

ACTIVITY:

OUTFIT:

SHOES:

ACC:

DAY: DESTINATION: PACKED: ☐

DAY: EVENING:

ACTIVITY:

OUTFIT:

SHOES:

ACC:

DAY: DESTINATION: PACKED: ☐

DAY: EVENING:

ACTIVITY:

OUTFIT:

SHOES:

ACC:

OUTFIT *Planner*

DAY: DESTINATION: PACKED: ☐

           DAY: EVENING:

ACTIVITY:

OUTFIT:

SHOES:

ACC:

DAY: DESTINATION: PACKED: ☐

           DAY: EVENING:

ACTIVITY:

OUTFIT:

SHOES:

ACC:

DAY: DESTINATION: PACKED:

           DAY: EVENING:

ACTIVITY:

OUTFIT:

SHOES:

ACC:

OUTFIT *Planner*

DAY:	DESTINATION:	PACKED: ☐

DAY:	EVENING:
ACTIVITY:	
OUTFIT:	
SHOES:	
ACC:	

DAY:	DESTINATION:	PACKED: ☐

DAY:	EVENING:
ACTIVITY:	
OUTFIT:	
SHOES:	
ACC:	

DAY:	DESTINATION:	PACKED: ☐

DAY:	EVENING:
ACTIVITY:	
OUTFIT:	
SHOES:	
ACC:	

OUTFIT *Planner*

DAY: DESTINATION: PACKED:

DAY: EVENING:

ACTIVITY:

OUTFIT:

SHOES:

ACC:

DAY: DESTINATION: PACKED:

DAY: EVENING:

ACTIVITY:

OUTFIT:

SHOES:

ACC:

DAY: DESTINATION: PACKED:

DAY: EVENING:

ACTIVITY:

OUTFIT:

SHOES:

ACC:

TRAVEL *Checklist*

DESTINATION: Luján de Cuyo   DATES:

NOTABLE TOWNS

Luján de Cuyo

Mendoza City

Chacras de Coria

Las Heras

POPULAR WINERIES

Bodega Carmelo Patti

Bodega Ruca Malen

Bodega Melipal

Bodego Vistalba

POPULAR HOTELS

Hotel & Spa Termas Cacheuta

Park Hyatt Mendoza

THINGS TO DO

Baccus Biking - Winery Tours

Parque San Martin

Aconcagua Provincial Park & Mt. Aconcagua

Peatonal Sarmiento

Reserva Natural Villavicencio

Carlos Alonso Museum – Stoppel House

Plaza Independencia

Museo de Ciencias Naturales y Antropológicas Juan Cornelio Moyano

White Water Rafting in Potrerillos

TRAVEL TIP:
Consider exploring the region by bike

WHERE TO EAT

Bodega Roberto Bonfanti

Casarena Bodega y Restaurante

Cava de Cano

HOTEL *Information*

NAME OF HOTEL:

ADDRESS:

PHONE NUMBER:

CONFIRMATION #:

CHECK IN/OUT:

ROOM TYPE:

RATE:

NAME OF HOTEL:

ADDRESS:

PHONE NUMBER:

CONFIRMATION #:

CHECK IN/OUT:

ROOM TYPE:

RATE:

NOTES

TRAVEL *Itinerary*

DESTINATION: DATE:

MON

TUE

WED

THU

FRI

SAT

SUN

VACATION *Planner*

DAILY ITINERARY

DATE: _____

LOCATION: _____

BUDGET: _____

TOP ACTIVITIES

MEAL PLANNER

TIME: SCHEDULE:

EXPENSES

TOTAL COST: _____

NOTES:

TRAVEL *Planner*

DATE:

DAY:

☀ ⛅ 🌧 ☁ ⛈

6	
7	
8	
9	
10	
11	
12	
1	
2	
3	
4	
5	
6	
7	
8	
9	
10	
11	
12	

NOTES

REMINDERS

VACATION *Planner*

DAILY ITINERARY

DATE: _____

LOCATION: _____

BUDGET: _____

TOP ACTIVITIES

MEAL PLANNER

TIME: SCHEDULE:

EXPENSES

TOTAL COST: _____

NOTES:

TRAVEL *Planner*

DATE:

☀ ⛅ 🌧 ☁ ⛈

6

7

8

9

10

11

12

1

2

3

4

5

6

7

8

9

10

11

12

DAY:

NOTES

REMINDERS

TRAVEL *Notes*

DATE: LOCATION:

DATE: LOCATION:

TRAVEL *Journal*

DATE: _____

_____

_____

_____

_____

_____

_____

_____

_____

_____

_____

_____

_____

_____

_____

_____

TRAVEL *Journal*

DATE: _____

_____

_____

_____

_____

_____

_____

_____

_____

_____

_____

_____

_____

_____

_____

WINE TASTING *Notes*

DATE: **TOWN:**

WINE NAME: **WINERY:**

TYPE OF GRAPE: **VINTAGE:**

APPEARANCE & SMELL:

TASTING NOTES: FLORAL   CITRUS   WOODSY   SPICE

PAIRING SUGGESTIONS:

FINAL RATING: ☆ ☆ ☆ ☆ ☆

TODAY'S FAVORITE MEMORIES:

WINE TASTING *Notes*

DATE: TOWN:

WINE NAME: **WINERY:**

TYPE OF GRAPE: **VINTAGE:**

APPEARANCE & SMELL:

TASTING NOTES: FLORAL   CITRUS   WOODSY   SPICE

PAIRING SUGGESTIONS:

FINAL RATING: ☆ ☆ ☆ ☆ ☆

TODAY'S FAVORITE MEMORIES:

WINE TASTING *Notes*

WINE NAME: **WINERY:**

TYPE OF GRAPE: **VINTAGE:**

APPEARANCE & SMELL:

TASTING NOTES: FLORAL   CITRUS   WOODSY   SPICE

PAIRING SUGGESTIONS:

FINAL RATING: ☆ ☆ ☆ ☆ ☆

TODAY'S FAVORITE MEMORIES:

WINE TASTING *Notes*

DATE: TOWN:

WINE NAME: **WINERY:**

TYPE OF GRAPE: **VINTAGE:**

APPEARANCE & SMELL:

TASTING NOTES: **FLORAL   CITRUS   WOODSY   SPICE**

PAIRING SUGGESTIONS:

FINAL RATING: ☆ ☆ ☆ ☆ ☆

TODAY'S FAVORITE MEMORIES:

TRAVEL *Journal*

DATE: _____

_____

_____

_____

_____

_____

_____

_____

_____

_____

_____

_____

_____

_____

_____

Bon Voyage

TRAVEL *Journal*

DATE: _____

_____

_____

_____

_____

_____

_____

_____

_____

_____

_____

_____

_____

_____

_____

_____

BEER TASTING *Notes*

DATE: **TOWN:**

BEER NAME: **BREWERY:**

TYPE OF HOPS: **TYPE OF BEER:**

APPEARANCE & BODY:

TASTING NOTES: HOPPY WOODSY CITRUS SOUR MALTY BITTER

PAIRING SUGGESTIONS:

FINAL RATING: ☆ ☆ ☆ ☆ ☆

TODAY'S FAVORITE MEMORIES:

BEER TASTING *Notes*

DATE: TOWN:

BEER NAME: BREWERY:

TYPE OF HOPS: TYPE OF BEER:

APPEARANCE & BODY:

TASTING NOTES: BITTER HOPPY CITRUS SOUR MALTY FLORAL

PAIRING SUGGESTIONS:

FINAL RATING: ☆ ☆ ☆ ☆ ☆

TODAY'S FAVORITE MEMORIES:

TRAVEL *Journal*

DATE: _____

_____
_____
_____
_____
_____
_____
_____
_____
_____
_____
_____
_____
_____
_____
_____

TRAVEL *Journal*

DATE: _____

_____

_____

_____

_____

_____

_____

_____

_____

_____

_____

_____

_____

_____

_____

_____

TRAVEL *Checklist*

DESTINATION: Uco Valley   **DATES:**

NOTABLE TOWNS

Tunuyán

San Carlos

Tupungato Region

Los Arboles

THINGS TO DO

Winery Tours

Taste Craft Beer at TRIBU Cervecería Artesanal y Café

Uco Valley Horseback Riding

Try Asado Beef

Spa Treatment at the Vines Resort

Take a Cooking Class

Excursion to Atuel Canyon

POPULAR WINERIES

Bodega la Azul

Bodegas Salentein

Bodega Andeluna

Bodega Zuccardi

Uco Valley Wines:
Sémillon, Malbec, Bonarda, & Barbera

POPULAR HOTELS

Tupungato Divino

Casa de Huespedes Finca La Azul

WHERE TO EAT

Arauco Restaurant

Atipana

7 Fuegos

HOTEL *Information*

NAME OF HOTEL:

ADDRESS:

PHONE NUMBER:

CONFIRMATION #:

CHECK IN/OUT:

ROOM TYPE:

RATE:

NAME OF HOTEL:

ADDRESS:

PHONE NUMBER:

CONFIRMATION #:

CHECK IN/OUT:

ROOM TYPE:

RATE:

NOTES

TRAVEL *Itinerary*

DESTINATION: DATE:

MON

TUE

WED

THU

FRI

SAT

SUN

VACATION *Planner*

DAILY ITINERARY

DATE: _____

LOCATION: _____

BUDGET: _____

TOP ACTIVITIES

MEAL PLANNER

TIME:

SCHEDULE:

EXPENSES

TOTAL COST: _____

NOTES:

TRAVEL *Planner*

DATE:

DAY:

6

7

8

9

10

11

12

1

2

3

4

5

6

7

8

9

10

11

12

NOTES

REMINDERS

VACATION *Planner*

DAILY ITINERARY

DATE: _____

LOCATION: _____

BUDGET: _____

TOP ACTIVITIES

MEAL PLANNER

TIME: SCHEDULE:

EXPENSES

TOTAL COST: _____

NOTES:

TRAVEL *Planner*

DATE:

DAY:

| 6 |
| 7 |
| 8 |
| 9 |
| 10 |
| 11 |
| 12 |
| 1 |
| 2 |
| 3 |
| 4 |
| 5 |
| 6 |
| 7 |
| 8 |
| 9 |
| 10 |
| 11 |
| 12 |

NOTES

REMINDERS

TRAVEL *Notes*

DATE: LOCATION:

DATE: LOCATION:

WINE TASTING *Notes*

DATE: TOWN:

WINE NAME: **WINERY:**

TYPE OF GRAPE: **VINTAGE:**

APPEARANCE & SMELL:

TASTING NOTES: **FLORAL   CITRUS   WOODSY   SPICY**

PAIRING SUGGESTIONS:

FINAL RATING: ☆ ☆ ☆ ☆ ☆

TODAY'S FAVORITE MEMORIES:

WINE TASTING *Notes*

DATE: TOWN:

WINE NAME: **WINERY:**

TYPE OF GRAPE: **VINTAGE:**

APPEARANCE & SMELL:

TASTING NOTES: FLORAL   CITRUS   WOODSY   SPICE

PAIRING SUGGESTIONS:

FINAL RATING: ☆ ☆ ☆ ☆ ☆

TODAY'S FAVORITE MEMORIES:

WINE TASTING *Notes*

WINE NAME: **WINERY:**

TYPE OF GRAPE: **VINTAGE:**

APPEARANCE & SMELL:

TASTING NOTES: **FLORAL   CITRUS   WOODSY   SPICE**

PAIRING SUGGESTIONS:

FINAL RATING: ☆ ☆ ☆ ☆ ☆

TODAY'S FAVORITE MEMORIES:

WINE TASTING *Notes*

DATE: TOWN:

WINE NAME: **WINERY:**

TYPE OF GRAPE: **VINTAGE:**

APPEARANCE & SMELL:

TASTING NOTES: FLORAL   CITRUS   WOODSY   SPICE

PAIRING SUGGESTIONS:

FINAL RATING: ☆ ☆ ☆ ☆ ☆

TODAY'S FAVORITE MEMORIES:

TRAVEL *Journal*

DATE: _____

TRAVEL *Journal*

DATE: _____

_____

_____

_____

_____

_____

_____

_____

_____

_____

_____

_____

_____

_____

_____

TRAVEL *Journal*

DATE: _____

_____

_____

_____

_____

_____

_____

_____

_____

_____

_____

_____

_____

_____

Bon Voyage

WINE TASTING *Notes*

DATE: TOWN:

WINE NAME: **WINERY:**

TYPE OF GRAPE: **VINTAGE:**

APPEARANCE & SMELL:

TASTING NOTES: FLORAL   CITRUS   WOODSY   SPICE

PAIRING SUGGESTIONS:

FINAL RATING: ☆ ☆ ☆ ☆ ☆

TODAY'S FAVORITE MEMORIES:

WINE TASTING *Notes*

DATE: TOWN:

WINE NAME: **WINERY:**

TYPE OF GRAPE: **VINTAGE:**

APPEARANCE & SMELL:

TASTING NOTES: **FLORAL   CITRUS   WOODSY   SPICE**

PAIRING SUGGESTIONS:

FINAL RATING:

TODAY'S FAVORITE MEMORIES:

TRAVEL *Journal*

DATE: _____

TRAVEL *Journal*

_____

_____

_____

_____

_____

_____

_____

_____

_____

_____

_____

_____

_____

TRAVEL *Checklist*

DESTINATION: Maipú   DATES:

LOCAL AREAS & TOWNS

Maipú

San Martin

POPULAR WINERIES

Bodegas López

Bodega Trapiche

Bodega Domiciano

Bodega Tempus Alba

POPULAR HOTELS

Posada Verde Oliva

Club Tapiz Hotel & Restó

THINGS TO DO

Winery Tours

Museo Nacional Del Vino y la Vendimia

Olive Oil Tours – The Olive Road

Maipú Region Wines:
Malbec, Cabernet, Pinot Noir

WHERE TO EAT

Bodega Santa Julia

Casa de Campo

Pie de Cuba

HOTEL *Information*

NAME OF HOTEL:

ADDRESS:

PHONE NUMBER:

CONFIRMATION #:

CHECK IN/OUT:

ROOM TYPE:

RATE:

NAME OF HOTEL:

ADDRESS:

PHONE NUMBER:

CONFIRMATION #:

CHECK IN/OUT:

ROOM TYPE:

RATE:

NOTES

TRAVEL *Itinerary*

DESTINATION: DATE:

MON

TUE

WED

THU

FRI

SAT

SUN

VACATION *Planner*

DAILY ITINERARY

DATE: _____

LOCATION: _____

BUDGET: _____

TOP ACTIVITIES

☀ ⛅ 🌧 ☁ ⛈

MEAL PLANNER

TIME: SCHEDULE:

EXPENSES

TOTAL COST: _____

NOTES:

TRAVEL *Planner*

DATE:

DAY:

NOTES

☀ ⛅ 🌦 ☁ ⛈

REMINDERS

6

7

8

9

10

11

12

1

2

3

4

5

6

7

8

9

10

11

12

TRAVEL *Planner*

DATE: DAY:

NOTES

☀ ⛅ 🌧 ☁ ⛈

6

7

8

9

10

11   REMINDERS

12

1

2

3

4

5

6

7

8

9

10

11

12

TRAVEL *Notes*

DATE: LOCATION:

DATE: LOCATION:

WINE TASTING *Notes*

DATE: TOWN:

WINE NAME: **WINERY:**

TYPE OF GRAPE: **VINTAGE:**

APPEARANCE & SMELL:

TASTING NOTES: FLORAL CITRUS WOODSY SPICE

PAIRING SUGGESTIONS:

FINAL RATING: ☆ ☆ ☆ ☆ ☆

TODAY'S FAVORITE MEMORIES:

WINE TASTING *Notes*

DATE: | TOWN:

WINE NAME: | **WINERY:**

TYPE OF GRAPE: | **VINTAGE:**

APPEARANCE & SMELL:

TASTING NOTES: **FLORAL**   **CITRUS**   **WOODSY**   **SPICE**

PAIRING SUGGESTIONS:

FINAL RATING: ☆ ☆ ☆ ☆ ☆

TODAY'S FAVORITE MEMORIES:

WINE TASTING *Notes*

DATE: TOWN:

WINE NAME: **WINERY:**

TYPE OF GRAPE: **VINTAGE:**

APPEARANCE & SMELL:

TASTING NOTES: FLORAL   CITRUS   WOODSY   SPICE

PAIRING SUGGESTIONS:

FINAL RATING:

TODAY'S FAVORITE MEMORIES:

WINE TASTING *Notes*

WINE NAME: **WINERY:**

TYPE OF GRAPE: **VINTAGE:**

APPEARANCE & SMELL:

TASTING NOTES: **FLORAL**   **CITRUS**   **WOODSY**   **SPICE**

PAIRING SUGGESTIONS:

FINAL RATING: ☆ ☆ ☆ ☆ ☆

TODAY'S FAVORITE MEMORIES:

TRAVEL *Journal*

DATE: _____

WINE TASTING *Notes*

DATE: TOWN:

WINE NAME: **WINERY:**

TYPE OF GRAPE: **VINTAGE:**

APPEARANCE & SMELL:

TASTING NOTES: FLORAL   CITRUS   WOODSY   SPICE

PAIRING SUGGESTIONS:

FINAL RATING: ☆ ☆ ☆ ☆ ☆

TODAY'S FAVORITE MEMORIES:

WINE TASTING *Notes*

DATE: TOWN:

WINE NAME: **WINERY:**

TYPE OF GRAPE: **VINTAGE:**

APPEARANCE & SMELL:

TASTING NOTES: **FLORAL**   **CITRUS**   **WOODSY**   **SPICE**

PAIRING SUGGESTIONS:

FINAL RATING: ☆ ☆ ☆ ☆ ☆

TODAY'S FAVORITE MEMORIES:

TRAVEL *Journal*

DATE: _____

TRAVEL *Journal*

DATE: _____

Bon Voyage

TRAVEL *Journal*

DATE: _____

_____

_____

_____

_____

_____

_____

_____

_____

_____

_____

_____

_____

_____

_____

TRAVEL *Journal*

DATE: _____

TRAVEL *Journal*

DATE: _____

Enjoy
every
moment

TRAVEL *Checklist*

DESTINATION:

DATES:

POPULAR HOTELS

THINGS TO DO

POPULAR WINERIES

RECOMMENDATIONS

WHERE TO EAT & DRINK

HOTEL *Information*

NAME OF HOTEL:

ADDRESS:

PHONE NUMBER:

CONFIRMATION #:

CHECK IN/OUT:

ROOM TYPE:

RATE:

NAME OF HOTEL:

ADDRESS:

PHONE NUMBER:

CONFIRMATION #:

CHECK IN/OUT:

ROOM TYPE:

RATE:

NOTES

TRAVEL *Itinerary*

DESTINATION: DATE:

MON

TUE

WED

THU

FRI

SAT

SUN

VACATION *Planner*

DAILY ITINERARY

DATE: _____

LOCATION: _____

BUDGET: _____

MEAL PLANNER

EXPENSES

_____ _____

_____ _____

_____ _____

_____ _____

_____ _____

TOTAL COST: _____

TOP ACTIVITIES

TIME:	SCHEDULE:

NOTES:

TRAVEL *Planner*

DATE:

DAY:

NOTES

6

7

8

9

10

11

REMINDERS

12

1

2

3

4

5

6

7

8

9

10

11

12

TRAVEL *Planner*

DATE:

DAY:

6

7

8

9

10

11

12

1

2

3

4

5

6

7

8

9

10

11

12

NOTES

REMINDERS

TRAVEL *Notes*

DATE: LOCATION:

DATE: LOCATION:

WINE TASTING *Notes*

DATE: TOWN:

WINE NAME: **WINERY:**

TYPE OF GRAPE: **VINTAGE:**

APPEARANCE & SMELL:

TASTING NOTES: FLORAL   CITRUS   WOODSY   SPICE

PAIRING SUGGESTIONS:

FINAL RATING: ☆ ☆ ☆ ☆ ☆

TODAY'S FAVORITE MEMORIES:

WINE TASTING *Notes*

DATE: TOWN:

WINE NAME: **WINERY:**

TYPE OF GRAPE: **VINTAGE:**

APPEARANCE & SMELL:

TASTING NOTES: FLORAL   CITRUS   WOODSY   SPICE

PAIRING SUGGESTIONS:

FINAL RATING: ☆ ☆ ☆ ☆ ☆

TODAY'S FAVORITE MEMORIES:

WINE TASTING *Notes*

DATE: TOWN:

WINE NAME: **WINERY:**

TYPE OF GRAPE: **VINTAGE:**

APPEARANCE & SMELL:

TASTING NOTES: **FLORAL**   **CITRUS**   **WOODSY**   **SPICE**

PAIRING SUGGESTIONS:

FINAL RATING: ☆ ☆ ☆ ☆ ☆

TODAY'S FAVORITE MEMORIES:

WINE TASTING *Notes*

DATE: TOWN:

WINE NAME: **WINERY:**

TYPE OF GRAPE: **VINTAGE:**

APPEARANCE & SMELL:

TASTING NOTES: FLORAL   CITRUS   WOODSY   SPICE

PAIRING SUGGESTIONS:

FINAL RATING: ☆ ☆ ☆ ☆ ☆

TODAY'S FAVORITE MEMORIES:

WINE TASTING *Notes*

DATE: TOWN:

WINE NAME: WINERY:

TYPE OF GRAPE: VINTAGE:

APPEARANCE & SMELL:

TASTING NOTES: FLORAL   CITRUS   WOODSY   SPICE

PAIRING SUGGESTIONS:

FINAL RATING: ☆ ☆ ☆ ☆ ☆

TODAY'S FAVORITE MEMORIES:

WINE TASTING *Notes*

DATE: TOWN:

WINE NAME: **WINERY:**

TYPE OF GRAPE: **VINTAGE:**

APPEARANCE & SMELL:

TASTING NOTES: FLORAL   CITRUS   WOODSY   SPICE

PAIRING SUGGESTIONS:

FINAL RATING: ☆ ☆ ☆ ☆ ☆

TODAY'S FAVORITE MEMORIES:

TRAVEL *Journal*

DATE: _____

_____

_____

_____

_____

_____

_____

_____

_____

_____

_____

_____

_____

_____

TRAVEL *Journal*

DATE: _____

TRAVEL *Journal*

DATE: _____

_____

_____

_____

_____

_____

_____

_____

_____

_____

_____

_____

_____

_____

_____

_____

Bon Voyage

TRAVEL *Checklist*

DESTINATION: DATES:

POPULAR HOTELS

THINGS TO DO

POPULAR WINERIES

RECOMMENDATIONS

WHERE TO EAT & DRINK

VACATION *Planner*

DAILY ITINERARY

DATE: _____

LOCATION: _____

BUDGET: _____

TOP ACTIVITIES

MEAL PLANNER

TIME: SCHEDULE:

EXPENSES

_____

_____

_____

_____

TOTAL COST: _____

NOTES:

TRAVEL *Planner*

DAY:

NOTES

6

7

8

9

10

11

12

REMINDERS

1

2

3

4

5

6

7

8

9

10

11

12

TRAVEL *Journal*

DATE: _____

WINE TASTING *Notes*

DATE: TOWN:

WINE NAME: **WINERY:**

TYPE OF GRAPE: **VINTAGE:**

APPEARANCE & SMELL:

TASTING NOTES: FLORAL   CITRUS   WOODSY   SPICE

PAIRING SUGGESTIONS:

FINAL RATING: ☆ ☆ ☆ ☆ ☆

TODAY'S FAVORITE MEMORIES:

WINE TASTING *Notes*

DATE: **TOWN:**

WINE NAME: **WINERY:**

TYPE OF GRAPE: **VINTAGE:**

APPEARANCE & SMELL:

TASTING NOTES: FLORAL   CITRUS   WOODSY   SPICE

PAIRING SUGGESTIONS:

FINAL RATING: ☆ ☆ ☆ ☆ ☆

TODAY'S FAVORITE MEMORIES:

WINE TASTING *Notes*

DATE: TOWN:

WINE NAME: **WINERY:**

TYPE OF GRAPE: **VINTAGE:**

APPEARANCE & SMELL:

TASTING NOTES: **FLORAL** **CITRUS** **WOODSY** **SPICE**

PAIRING SUGGESTIONS:

FINAL RATING: ☆ ☆ ☆ ☆ ☆

TODAY'S FAVORITE MEMORIES:

WINE TASTING *Notes*

DATE: TOWN:

WINE NAME: **WINERY:**

TYPE OF GRAPE: **VINTAGE:**

APPEARANCE & SMELL:

TASTING NOTES: FLORAL   CITRUS   WOODSY   SPICE

PAIRING SUGGESTIONS:

FINAL RATING: ☆ ☆ ☆ ☆ ☆

TODAY'S FAVORITE MEMORIES:

TRAVEL *Journal*

DATE: _____

TRAVEL *Journal*

DATE: _____

TRAVEL *Checklist*

DESTINATION: DATES:

POPULAR HOTELS

THINGS TO DO

POPULAR WINERIES

RECOMMENDATIONS

WHERE TO EAT & DRINK

HOTEL *Information*

HOTEL INFORMATION

NAME OF HOTEL:

ADDRESS:

PHONE NUMBER:

CONFIRMATION #:

CHECK IN/OUT:

ROOM TYPE:

RATE:

HOTEL INFORMATION

NAME OF HOTEL:

ADDRESS:

PHONE NUMBER:

CONFIRMATION #:

CHECK IN/OUT:

ROOM TYPE:

RATE:

NOTES

TRAVEL *Itinerary*

DESTINATION: DATE:

MON

TUE

WED

THU

FRI

SAT

SUN

VACATION *Planner*

DAILY ITINERARY

DATE: _____

LOCATION: _____

BUDGET: _____

TOP ACTIVITIES

MEAL PLANNER

TIME: SCHEDULE:

EXPENSES

TOTAL COST: _____

NOTES:

TRAVEL *Planner*

DATE: DAY:

NOTES

☀ ⛅ 🌦 ☁ ⛈

6

7

8

9

10

11   REMINDERS

12

1

2

3

4

5

6

7

8

9

10

11

12

TRAVEL *Planner*

DATE:

DAY:

	NOTES

6

7

8

9

10

11

12

1

2

3

	REMINDERS

4

5

6

7

8

9

10

11

12

TRAVEL *Notes*

DATE: LOCATION:

DATE: LOCATION:

WINE TASTING *Notes*

DATE: TOWN:

WINE NAME: **WINERY:**

TYPE OF GRAPE: **VINTAGE:**

APPEARANCE & SMELL:

TASTING NOTES: FLORAL   CITRUS   WOODSY   SPICE

PAIRING SUGGESTIONS:

FINAL RATING: ☆ ☆ ☆ ☆ ☆

TODAY'S FAVORITE MEMORIES:

WINE TASTING *Notes*

DATE: TOWN:

WINE NAME: **WINERY:**

TYPE OF GRAPE: **VINTAGE:**

APPEARANCE & SMELL:

TASTING NOTES: FLORAL   CITRUS   WOODSY   SPICE

PAIRING SUGGESTIONS:

FINAL RATING: ☆ ☆ ☆ ☆ ☆

TODAY'S FAVORITE MEMORIES:

WINE TASTING *Notes*

DATE: TOWN:

WINE NAME: **WINERY:**

TYPE OF GRAPE: **VINTAGE:**

APPEARANCE & SMELL:

TASTING NOTES: **FLORAL**   **CITRUS**   **WOODSY**   **SPICE**

PAIRING SUGGESTIONS:

FINAL RATING: ☆ ☆ ☆ ☆ ☆

TODAY'S FAVORITE MEMORIES:

WINE TASTING *Notes*

DATE: TOWN:

WINE NAME: **WINERY:**

TYPE OF GRAPE: **VINTAGE:**

APPEARANCE & SMELL:

TASTING NOTES: **FLORAL   CITRUS   WOODSY   SPICE**

PAIRING SUGGESTIONS:

FINAL RATING: ☆ ☆ ☆ ☆ ☆

TODAY'S FAVORITE MEMORIES:

TRAVEL *Journal*

DATE: _____

TRAVEL *Journal*

DATE: _____

_____

_____

_____

_____

_____

_____

_____

_____

_____

_____

_____

_____

_____

TRAVEL *Journal*

DATE: _____

_____

_____

_____

_____

_____

_____

_____

_____

_____

_____

_____

_____

_____

_____

TRAVEL *Journal*

DATE: _____

_____
_____
_____
_____
_____
_____
_____
_____
_____
_____
_____
_____
_____
_____
_____